bringing up baby:

the movie lover's guide to parents and parenthood

bringing up baby:

the movie lover's guide to parents and parenthood

jim poling

Kensington Books

http://www.kensingtonbooks.com

KENSINGTON BOOKS are published by

Kensington Publishing Corp.
850 Third Avenue
New York, NY 10022

ISBN 1-57566-147-0

First Printing: March, 1997
10 9 8 7 6 5 4 3 2 1

Printed in the United States of America

*Dedicated to my mother,
who brought me up at
the Ottowa Drive-in.*

"For as long as I can remember, the house on Larkin Street had become home. Papa and Mama had both been born in Norway, but they came to San Francisco because Mama's sisters were here. I remember it all . . . But first and foremost . . . I remember Mama."

> —Barbara Bel Geddes's touching tribute to Irene Dunne in *I Remember Mama*

"If my father was the head of our house, my mother was its heart."

> —Irving Pichel in *How Green Was My Valley*

"Your father was Frankenstein . . . but your mother was the lightning!"

> —Bela Lugosi, electrifying, in *The Ghost of Frankenstein*

"Be a parent . . . *not* a policeman."

—Motherly advice from Sophia Loren to Cary Grant in *Houseboat*

"To lose one parent may be regarded as a misfortune, to lose both looks like carelessness."

—Edith Evans to orphan Michael Redgrave in
The Importance of Being Earnest

"We've got a 23-year-old boy . . . presumably building bombs in basements as an expression of his universal brotherhood. We've got a 17-year-old daughter who's had two abortions in two years. Got arrested last week at a rock festival for pushing drugs. A typical affluent American family."

—George C. Scott's bitter confession in *The Hospital*

"My mother and father together are like a bad car wreck."

—Al Pacino in *Dog Day Afternoon*

"Such a bother over a few drops of semen."

—Jill Clayburgh to Gabriel Byrne in *Hanna K.*

"Believe you me, if it didn't take men to make babies I wouldn't have anything to do with any of you."

—Gena Rowlands on the male gender in
Lonely Are the Brave

"There are two types of women in this world who get accidentally pregnant: idiots and liars."

—Francis Fisher in *Babyfever*

"The way they always made us feel . . . like we were the two most important, smartest, talented, most handsomest . . . And it kills me to think they look at me and wonder what they did wrong."

—Harvey Fierstein shares his fears to his brother that he isn't all his parents hoped he would be in *Torch Song Trilogy*

"It's because he was our first. I mean I think we were very tense when Kevin was little. If he got a scratch we were hysterical. By the third kid, you know, you let 'em juggle knives."

—Mary Steenburgen's theory on why her son is too tense, in *Parenthood*

"That child is mine. Your part was finished the minute you gave that baby to me. From that day on I had only one purpose in my life—to make that baby mine and forget you ever existed!"

—Bette Davis to birth-mother Mary Astor in *The Great Lie*

"The book says to feed the baby every two hours, but do you count from when you start, or when you finish? It takes me two hours to get her to eat, and by the time she's done, it's time to start again . . . I'm feeding her all the time!"

—Exasperated Tom Selleck in *Three Men and a Baby*

"Children are mankind at his strongest . . . they abide."

—Earthmother Lillian Gish in *The Night of the Hunter*

"They like the idea of having children, but they were never very interested in raising them."

> —Barbara Hershey on her parents in *Hannah and Her Sisters*

"Daughters! They're a mess no matter how you look at 'em. A headache till they get married . . . and after that they get worse . . . Either they leave their husbands and come with four kids and move in your guest room . . . Or else they're so homely that you can't get rid of them at all and they sit around like Spanish moss and shame you into an early grave."

> —Actually quite lovable William Demarest in *The Miracle of Morgan's Creek*

"Don't you ever hit her, and don't you take her away from home."

> —Protective papa Levon Helm to his future son-in-law in *Coal Miner's Daughter*

"Polly . . . when I grow up I want to be just like you!"

> —Down and out mother Marsha Mason to her sensible daughter in *Only When I Laugh*

"I'm a father, worry comes with the territory."

—Steve Martin as *Father of the Bride*

"I don't want to adopt, no . . . with my genes? I have award-winning genes. The same reason we don't lease a car—pride of ownership."

—Woody Allen, shortly before adopting, in *Mighty Aphrodite*

"That's the trouble with mothers . . . you get to like them and they die."

—Kay Francis in *Trouble in Paradise*

"This kid is gonna be a great kid. What do you want to call him? I want to name him after one of my heros. What about Groucho? I just want the kid to have a great name. What about Sugar Ray Weinrich . . . what about Cole? Cole Weinrich . . . Harpo Weinrich. What about Earl 'The Pearl' Weinrich? That would be so perfect."

—Woody Allen, before settling on "Max," in *Mighty Aphrodite*

"My mother's a Jezebel. She's so overloaded with sex that it sparkles! She's golden and striped like something in the jungle!"

—Imaginative Hayley Mills in *The Chalk Garden*

"Any man who has lived as I have and indulges for the first time in parenthood at the age of 55 deserves all he gets."

—Charles Waldron, not liking what he got, in
The Big Sleep

"In this day and age every woman ought to know how to get pregnant and how *not* to get pregnant. It's only forty-eight hours a month—no big deal—that you keep your legs closed."

—Francis Fisher on how to avoid *Babyfever*

"There'll be one thousand dollars on that table for you by six in the morning. Get on the early train. Send a Christmas card each year to an aging parent who now wishes you to stop talking."

—Contemptible Frederic March to his son
Dan Duryea in *Another Part of the Forest*

"How do you explain to your daughter, she was born to be hurt?"

—Juanita Moore in *Imitation of Life*

"Top of the world, Ma!"

> —Explosive tribute from James Cagney in
> *White Heat*

"Teenagers by definition are not fit for society."

> —Nick Nolte on Barbra Streisand's horrid son
> in *The Prince of Tides*

"Nice, clean middle class girls do not rub elbows—or anything else—with nasty, dirty lower class boys."

> —No amount of motherly advice by Joanna
> Merlin is going to keep her daughter
> Rosanna Arquette away from Vincent Spano
> in *Baby It's You*

"The world is filled with what-you-call-em?—schlemiels—and I guess somebody has to raise 'em."

> —Victor Moore on his ungrateful children in
> *Make Way for Tomorrow*

"Tonight, just tonight, she belongs to me! Tonight I want her to call me Mommy."

> —Bette Davis's wish in *The Old Maid*

"You're no more my mother than a toad."

> —Gene Tierney denying her heritage in *The Shanghai Gesture*

"I'm not his mother . . . not really. Just bringing a child into the world doesn't make you that. It's being there . . ."

> —Olivia de Havilland in *To Each His Own*

"A boy's best friend is his mother."

> —And sometimes one and the same. Anthony Perkins in *Psycho*

"You know what I do sometimes? When I'm shopping I see baby clothes that are on sale that are really cute and I buy them and I take them home and put them in a box . . . and I think this is crazy, I don't even have a baby."

> —Victoria Foyt planning for *Babyfever*

"It's such a joy to be a mother! It's such a joy and I thank God for letting me know it!"

> —Kate Nelligan in *Eleni*

"My mother should have raised cobras—not children."

> —Nick Nolte in *The Prince of Tides*

"Unsuitable? Don't you dare judge me . . . obviously you don't understand. What you're really doing is denying one of your children the opportunity to live a wonderful and advantaged life. How sad that is."

> —Faye Dunaway to the adoption board on
> her qualifications for motherhood in
> *Mommie Dearest*

"It sure would be nice to have a mother that somebody liked."

> —Debra Winger, regretfully, in *Terms of Endearment*

"*Bonanza* is about a fifty-seven-year-old father and his three forty-seven-year-old sons. What kind of show is that?"

> —Amateur TV critic Jackie Gayle in *Tin Men*

"All my sons are bastards."

> —A legitimate beef for Peter O'Toole in *The Lion in Winter*

"[He is] the bastard son of a thousand maniacs."

> —Ronee Blakely on Freddie Kruger's bloodline in *A Nightmare on Elm Street*

"You know how I got you Marnie? There was this boy, Billy. And I wanted Billy's basketball sweater. I was fifteen. And Billy said if I . . . 'let him' I could have his sweater. So I let him. And later on, when *you* got started, he ran away. I still got that old sweater. And I got *you* Marnie."

> —Louise Latham gets to the root of her daughter Tippi Hedrin's problems in *Marnie*

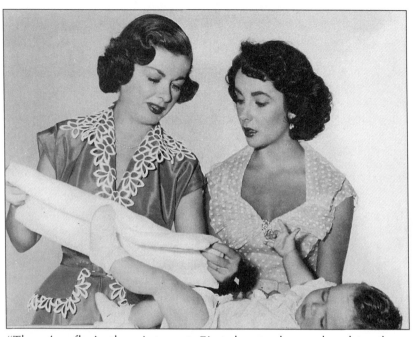

"There's a fly in the ointment. First, he steals my daughter then he makes a grandpa out of me!"

—Spencer Tracy in *Father's Little Dividend*

"Fly, may I call you Mom?"

—A request from *Babe* the pig to a pupless sheepdog that satisfies both their needs.

"I refuse to endanger the health of my children in a house with less than four bathrooms!"

> —A demanding Myrna Loy in *Mr. Blanding Builds His Dreamhouse*

"I had a man around. He used to wake me up by flickin' lit cigarettes at my head. You know . . . you need a license to buy a dog, or drive a car—hell, you need a license to catch a fish. But they'll let any butt-reamin' asshole be a father."

> —Keanu Reaves, on the consequences of bad father-figuring, in *Parenthood*

"Give me a girl at an impressionable age . . . and she's mine for life."

> —Maternal Maggie Smith in *The Prime of Miss Jean Brodie*

"I'm just your mother. You only owe me your entire existence on this planet!"

> —Elizabeth Wilson giving *The Addams Family* stiff competition in creepiness

"She's always been a happy human being. She laughed out loud before she was six months old. She was happy as a baby . . . happiest little girl. But I don't think I've ever seen her as happy as she is right now. And I have to be happy for her . . . I feel happy for her—and proud of the fact that we helped make her . . ."

> —Katharine Hepburn to Spencer Tracy, accepting of her daughter's decision to marry a black man, in *Guess Who's Coming to Dinner?*

"I'm fat! My mother doesn't approve of dieting. Look at my shoes. My mother approves of sensible shoes. Look at the books on my shelves. My mother approves of good, solid books. I am my mother's well-loved daughter. I am her companion. I am my mother's servant. My mother. My mother. *My mother!*"

> —Bette Davis finally lets go in *Now, Voyager*

"I'll never forget it. Never as long as I live. She said 'Mommy' and that was all . . ."

> —Joan Crawford remembering her lost daughter in *Mildred Pierce*

"Every time an egg is released . . . there's a little scar tissue on the outside of the ovary and an egg can never be released from that area again, so your ovaries become like these dried-up raisins. They become this scar-tissued little nut by the time you're forty—just when you want to have kids."

> —Cindy Friedl, not exactly the voice of hope, to a table of forty-year-old women in *Babyfever*

"Death ends a life, but it does not end a relationship which struggles on in the survivor's mind toward some resolution which it never finds. What did it matter if I never loved him or he never loved me? . . . But still, when I hear the word 'Father' . . . it matters."

> —Gene Hackman's restitution after the death of his father in *I Never Sang for My Father*

"I can see your dirty pillows."
"Breasts, Mama."

> —Piper Laurie and daughter Sissy Spacek, not the healthiest of relationships, in *Carrie*

"Today, I have a son. What a joy."

> —Lana Turner's dying words as *Madame X*

"You know who I work for? My son is going to be all right. If not . . . I'll have you killed."

> —Monster mommy Angelica Huston to a
> team of doctors in *The Grifters*

"She told me she thinks I'm a son of a bitch. She also thinks I'm a funny son of a bitch. She loves me but she doesn't like me. She's afraid of me, she's intimidated by me. She respects me, but she doesn't want to become like me. We have a perfectly normal mother-daughter relationship."

> —Jane Fonda in *California Suite*

"Every time I try to get close to you, you push me away. How would you like to have Joan Crawford for a mother?"

> —Shirley MacLaine in *Postcards from the Edge*

"Anything you do is wrong. If you spruce yourself up it's 'Oh mother that's too kiddish for you.' If you don't it's 'Mother, do you have to dress like an old bag?' . . . And if anything goes wrong, they turn back to being six or seven years old and clinging to you. And that's heaven!"

> —Mildred Natwick on the trials of having
> teenagers, in *Teenage Rebel*

"I *can't* have a baby . . . I have a 12:30 lunch meeting!"

—Diane Keaton in *Baby Boom*

"When I told you to call me that . . . I wanted you to mean it!"

> —Faye Dunaway as Joan Crawford upon hearing . . . *Mommie Dearest*

"Personally, Veda's convinced me that alligators have the right idea—they eat their young."

> —Eve Arden to Joan Crawford in *Mildred Pierce*

"She's my sister *and* my daughter!"

> —Faye Dunaway in *Chinatown*

"There won't be no patter of little feet in my house—unless I was to rent some mice."

> —Tough-talking Peggy Lee in *Pete Kelley's Blues*

"I'm too young . . . Grandmothers are old. They bake and sew and they tell you stories about the Depression. I was at Woodstock, for Christ's sake! I peed in a field! I've hung on to the Who's helicopter as it flew away!"

> —Dianne Wiest questioning her motherhood capabilities in *Parenthood*

"One man is as good as the next. And even the least accommodating is less trouble than a mother."

> —Glenn Close in *Dangerous Liaisons*

"Tell me, why is it doctors and nurses and husbands always seem to think they know more about this maternity business? Don't you think a mother learns anything in that little room they wheel 'em into? Let me tell you something . . . I picked up a lot of experience in that room, and it wasn't out of books, either."

> —Barbara Stanwyck as martyr mother *Stella Dallas*

"You mustn't kid Mother, dear. I was a married woman before you were born."

> —Lucille Watson wanting the truth from her daughter Norma Shearer in *The Women*

"I watched you with that baby—that other woman's baby. You looked . . . well, nice."

> —John Wayne admiring the less-than-maternal Claire Trevor in *Stagecoach*

"I'm an okay sort of person. How did I get such a smart-ass kid?"

—Ellen Burstyn in *Alice Doesn't Live Here Anymore*

"Ah don't know nothin' 'bout birthin' babies!"

—Butterfly McQueen fesses up in *Gone with the Wind*

"Babies come from when an angel lights on their mother's chest and whispers into her ear. That makes good babies start to grow. Bad babies come from when a fallen angel squeezes in down there and they grow and grow until they come out down there."

—Meg Tilly, not exactly ready for motherhood in *Agnes of God*

"A dingo stole my baby!"

—Excuses, excuses. Meryl Streep in *A Cry in the Dark*

"How is your life going to get any better if you're going to keep having children with man?"

—Disapproving Shirley MacLaine to daughter Debra Winger in *Terms of Endearment*

"You know when your kid is born, he can still be perfect. You haven't made any mistakes yet. Then they grow up to be like . . . *me.*"

—Steve Martin, on the unavoidable pains of
Parenthood

"I'm not young and I'm not glowing. I'm fat."

> —Dinah Lenney getting *Babyfever*

"My children are the spawn of hell."

> —Goldie Hawn goes *Overboard*

"I bet your father spent the first years of your life throwing rocks at the stork."

> —Groucho Marx to Eve Arden in *At the Circus*

"All I wanted was a father—not a boss!"

> —Paul Newman to Big Daddy in *Cat on a Hot Tin Roof*

"So much for Mrs. Hollis's nine months of pain and twenty years of hope."

> —Sad eulogy from John Whitney upon finding his buddy's body in *Objective Burma*

"I would like to adopt every unwanted child in the world! No one should be unwanted. Life is tough enough when you *are* wanted."

—New mother Faye Dunaway in *Mommie Dearest*

"I put a crimp in her career . . . but that's alright because she gives me . . . an autographed picture of herself for my birthday, signed 'Sincerely, Gertrude Vanderhof.' It comes from the studio mailing room. It seems they've got me mixed up with one of her fans."

> —Lee Kinsolving, bitterly, about Mama, in
> *The Dark at the Top of the Stairs*

"You think mother is a dirty word!"

> —Angela Lansbury to son Warren Beatty in
> *All Fall Down*

"Go, desert me! When I was expecting him in the maternity ward, three days I waited. Did I desert him? No. I stayed right there so he wouldn't be alone when he was born!"

> —Maureen Stapleton complaining to Paul
> Lynde about her "thankless" son in *Bye Bye
> Birdie*

"You belong to me. If I could stuff you, I'd put you in the cabinet there, along with my other beautiful possessions. *That's* [a mother's] love!"

> —The biggest mother of them all, Bette Davis,
> in *The Anniversary*

"You say you don't want to tell me how to live my life? So what do you think you've been doing? You tell me what rights I've got—or haven't got, and what I owe to *you* for what you've done for *me.* Let me tell you something. I owe you nothing . . . because you brought me into this world. And from that day *you* owed *me* everything you could ever do for me like I will owe my son . . ."

> —Sidney Poitier telling his father to get off his back in *Guess Who's Coming to Dinner?*

"Love!? But you've always had that!"
"Yes—by telephone, by postcard, by magazine interviews. You've given me everything—but yourself!"

> —Lana Turner's imitation of motherhood for Sandra Dee in *Imitation of Life*

"I'll do anything for those kids. Do you understand? *Anything!*"

> —Almost. Accommodating Joan Crawford as *Mildred Pierce*

"Had I been sterile, darling, I'd be happier today."

> —Katharine Hepburn to her son in *The Lion in Winter*

29

"Oh please, let me see her face when he kisses her."

—Barbara Stanwyck's last wish, granted, as
the martyr mother of all time, *Stella Dallas,*
on her daughter's wedding day

"Don't you think everyone looks back on their childhood with a certain amount of bitterness and regret about something? It doesn't have to ruin your life, darling. You're a big girl now . . . life marches on . . . I suggest you get on *with* it."

> —Katharine Hepburn's words of advice to bitter and regretful daughter Jane Fonda in *On Golden Pond*

"You see, [my husband] understood the children. He really understood them. He had the knack of entering their world and becoming part of them. That's a very rare talent . . . Oh, I wish I wish I wish I could be like that."

> —Jessica Tandy mourning her husband—and his way with their kids—in *The Birds*

"Nobody laughs at me, because I laugh first—at me. *Me,* from Seattle, *me* with no education, *me* with no talent, as you kept reminding me my whole life. Well, Mama, look at me now. I'm a star . . . I'm having the time of my life. Because for the first time in my life it *is* my life, and I love it. I love every second of it, and I'll be damned if you're gonna take it away from me!"

> —Natalie Wood finally cuts the apron strings, in *Gypsy*

"Father + divorce × guilt = sweaters."

> —Roddy McDowall gives Tuesday Weld the equation on tooling her father for cashmere sweaters, in *Lord Love a Duck*

"I'm doing a lot for my kids. I don't expect them to pay me back at the end."

> —Estelle Parsons, unconditionally, in *I Never Sang for My Father*

"These are my children. They were born in India, poor darlings. An awful place . . . Of course, I've never been there myself."

> —Mother Billie Burke introducing her son and daughter in *The Young in Heart*

"I love my children. But they are not the only children in the world."

> —Paul Lukas clarifying the boundaries of fatherhood in *Watch on the Rhine*

"What's the point of having a dwarf if he doesn't do chores?"

> —Henry Fonda, lovably hateful, in *On Golden Pond*

"I was an unwelcomed child in a marriage which was a nice imitation of hell . . . indifference, fear, infidelity and guilt feelings—these were my nurses."

> —Gunnar Björnstrand bringing down the party in *Wild Strawberries*

"I just fainted in the subway, but I didn't fall down—it was too crowded . . . Taxis are for my successful son. A dirty, crowded subway is good enough for a mother. Mothers are nothing nowadays."

> —Maureen Stapleton shovelling on the guilt in *Bye Bye Birdie*

"Everything in [my mother's] behavior toward me as a little boy seemed to say: I'd have done better to break a leg than to give birth to this stupid child."

> —Charles Denner as *The Man Who Loved Women*—some of them.

"I'd like to help but I really don't like children. Especially yours."

> —Surrogate mother Gena Rowlands refusing to hide a young boy from gangsters in *Gloria*

"What law is it that says a woman is a better parent simply by virtue of her sex? I've had to think a lot about whatever it is that makes somebody a good parent—constancy, patience, understanding . . . love. Where is it written that a man has less of those qualities than a woman?"

—Good point from Dustin Hoffman in *Kramer vs. Kramer*

"Sure you'll help me . . . right over a cliff you'll help me . . . never you mind those angelic faces—I know vixen when I see 'em. Just remember this—you start anything and I will make your lives just miserable for you later on. You get me, pets?"

—Wicked step-mother-to-be Joanna Barnes, outnumbered by Hayley Mills X 2 in *The Parent Trap*

"Why any kid would want to be an orphan is beyond me."

> —A sneering Carol Burnett to the little orphan
> *Annie*

"I'm what became of your child."

> —Unhappy pronouncement from daughter
> Sissy Spacek to mother Anne Bancroft in
> *'Night Mother*

"The only wealth is children. More than power or money."

> —Al Pacino in *The Godfather, Part II*

"Sons . . . my eldest, a penny-grubbing trickster . . . my second, a proud illiterate. Strange, Regina, you turned out to be my only son."

> —Frederic March to daughter Ann Blythe in
> *Another Part of the Forest*

"Every father's daughter is a virgin."

> —Blind wisdom from *Goodbye, Columbus*

"[You are] nothing but a ball and chain of heartbreak and hurt."

> —Monstrous Maureen O'Hara to son John
> Candy in *Only the Lonely*

"I have thought I heard you say, 'twas a pity I never had any children. But I have . . . thousands of them . . . and all boys."

> —Robert Donat, on his deathbed, in *Goodbye Mr. Chips*

"Oh Sebastian. What a lovely summer it's been. Just the two of us. Sebastian and Violet, Violet and Sebastian. Just the way it's always going to be. Oh, we are lucky, my darling, to have one another and need no one else ever."

> —Demented mother Katharine Hepburn on her love for her son in *Suddenly, Last Summer*

"You look like kids, but you don't act like it. You're short 40-year-olds."

> —Sally Kellerman to her daughter Jodie Foster, and pals, in *Foxes*

"I came here to take my son home. And I realized he already is home."

> —Meryl Streep, finally recognizing the truth, in *Kramer vs. Kramer*

"I won't have you bringing strange young girls in here for supper by candlelight, I suppose, in the cheap, erotic fashion of young men with cheap, erotic minds . . . Go tell her she'll not be appeasing her ugly appetite with my food or my son! Or do I have to tell her 'cause you don't have the guts!?"

—Mother, not quite herself, in *Psycho*

"Next time I have a daughter . . . I hope it's a boy."

—Paul Lynde, exasperated with daughter Ann-Margret in *Bye Bye Birdie*

"You come from good stock. Your grandmother snuck across the Polish border buried under sacks of potatoes. The guards put bayonets into the sacks, but she never cried out. That's where you come from!"

—Mama Shelly Winters stressing to stressed-out son in *Next Stop, Greenwich Village*

"A motel mattress full of lumps is good enough for me. Comfort is for my loving son."

—Maureen Stapleton in *Bye Bye Birdie*

"I'm too selfish to do it . . . I just can't do it. My breasts will never get big enough . . . I can't even conceive of the fact of someone growing inside me. It freaks me out."

> —Victoria Foyt, who's about to learn the inconceivable, in *Babyfever*

"That miserable little brat. She is becoming impossible—simply impossible. The idea—the idea of her sneaking back here and spying on us . . . She's always been a spiteful little pest since the age of one. Do you know she kept throwing her toys out of her crib so that I would have to keep stooping over to pick them up? She has always had some kind of gripe against me. Now—now she sees herself as some kind of starlet. Well, I see her as a sturdy, healthy, but decidedly homely child!"

> —Shelly Winters, indignant and insecure, over her daughter, *Lolita*

"The happiest days are when babies come."

> —Olivia de Havilland, gushing, in *Gone with the Wind*

"My daddy used to say there's a special God for children."

> —A grateful Mary Louise Parker in *Fried Green Tomatoes*

"It's smart to have babies when you're young—before you get funky."

<blockquote>
—Joan Cusack to Jessica Lange in Men Don't Leave
</blockquote>

"I always thought I could give them life like a present, all wrapped in white with every promise of happiness. All I can promise them is life itself."

<blockquote>
—Dorothy McGuire resigned to . . . life, in The Dark at the Top of the Stairs
</blockquote>

"She can love whom she pleases, but she must marry the man I choose."

<blockquote>
—Hugh Griffith, exhibiting control in Tom Jones
</blockquote>

"Suppose your parents are unhappy—it's good for them. It develops their characters. Now look at me. I left home at the age of four, and I haven't been back since. They can hear me on the radio, and that's enough for them."

<blockquote>
—We can well imagine. Monty Woolley in The Man Who Came to Dinner
</blockquote>

"If I had ever opened a mouth to my mother the way you did to me you'd be talkin' to a woman with a size 6 wedgie stickin' out of her forehead."

> —Anne Bancroft, in need of a size 6 wedgie stickin' out of her forehead, to her son in *Torch Song Trilogy*

"When I was four years old, my old man ran away . . . I used to dream about getting rich someday—rich enough to hire a detective to find my father. And then I was going to beat his head off. You know . . . kid stuff."

> —Kirk Douglas in *Champion*

"Beware of the children."

> —Ma and Pa Kettle's stern warning in *The Egg and I*

"Do you sleep in the same room with her?"
"Sure. How else can I be a lesbian?"
"Where does [your son] sleep? . . . In the same bed? Is that a way to bring up a boy? He'll be a lesbian!"

> —Irrational grandma Sylvia Miles, horrified by her daughter's lovelife in *Heat*

"Whistles are for dogs and cats but not for children . . . It would be too humiliating."

—Julie Andrews letting Christopher Plummer have it in *The Sound of Music*

"You know when you were two years old we thought you had polio? For a week, we didn't know. I hated you for that . . . I hated having to go through that . . . the worrying, the pain—It's not for me. It's not like it all ends when you're 18 or 21 or 41 or 61. It *never never* ends. It's like your Aunt Edna's ass . . . it goes on forever and it's just as frightening."

> —Jason Robards preparing his son Steve Martin for the lifelong worrying and pain of *Parenthood*

"I'm 36 years old, I have a wife, a child and a mortgage, and I'm scared to death that I'm turning into my father . . . Something tells me this may be my last chance to do something about it."

> —Kevin Costner fulfills his—and his father's— dreams in *Field of Dreams*

"Some women were born to have a *baby."*

> —Lily Pons, choosing motherhood upon being told she was "born to sing" in *I Dream Too Much*

"You're in your green years, Robbie. You suffer the critical disease of being young. The Lord deliver me from ever having to go through that again!"

> —Charles Coburn, attempting to comfort his troubled grandson in *The Green Years*

"My father taught me many things . . . Keep your friends close, but your enemies closer."

> —Good advice for Al Pacino in *The Godfather, Part III*

"My mother . . . was a little bit of a thing . . . died when I was 10. I don't remember much about her funeral, except my father. He'd run out on us, but he came back when she died, but I wouldn't let him come to the cemetery. Little bit of a thing . . ."

> —Melvyn Douglas reminded of his mother, by the death of his wife, in *I Never Sang for My Father*

"You *are* your father's daughter."

> —Not a compliment, coming from Constance Ford to "loose moraled" daughter Sandra Dee in *A Summer Place*

"Mother, I think what you and daddy did to us children is lousy! In fact I think it stinks! And let's get this straight . . . I'm *not* Sharon . . . I'm Susan!"

> —Hayley Mills, masquerading as her twin sister in *The Parent Trap*

"Where did you get that outfit? It's a new garment, Lulu, I can smell it. Have you been shoplifting again?"

> —Put-upon mother Divine to her slutty daughter Mary Garlington in *Polyester*

"[Men] call up and they're very nice and they say 'would you like to go out to dinner?' and I say 'dinner?' I've gone to dinner for years and it's done no good. *I have to have a child!*"

> —The clock ticks for Irene Forest in *Babyfever*

"I'm somebody! I'm the mother of a famous man! I'm a celebrity!"

> —Mama Shelly Winters upon realizing her son is a renowned neo-Nazi rock star in *Wild in the Streets*

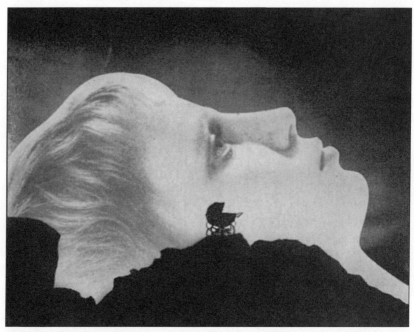

"Why don't you help us out, Rosemary? Be a *real* mother to Adrian . . . be a mother to your baby . . . think about it."

—A tall order for Mia Farrow from Sidney Blackmer in *Rosemary's Baby*

"My mother? Don't waste your time. She ditched us when I was 11 and ran off with some motel man in the east. *You* know what a mother's love is."

"Yes, I do."

"You mean it's better to be ditched . . ."

> —Tippi Hedrin exposes her mother
> problems—and Rod Taylor's mother
> problems—in *The Birds*

"She's not like an automobile or an icebox or a piece of furniture or something that you buy on time and then when you can't keep up the payments they take it away from you. Anyone can give up those things. But I ask you, judge, how can you give up your own child?"

> —Cary Grant pleads his case for his adopted
> daughter in *Penny Serenade*

"You've been sound and sweet and loving! You've given me more than I could ever repay . . . you knew nothing but love and kindness from us and you've given love and kindness, and sweetness all your life . . . And Rhoda's a perfect, sweet, sound little girl!"

"Is she, Father . . . *is she?!*"

> —A resounding "NO!" for Nancy Kelly, mother
> of Patty McCormack, in *The Bad Seed*

"The family that slays together, stays together."

— The heartwarming motto of Shelly Winters
as *Bloody Mama*

"Living with an illegitimate child is wrong and unnatural . . . It will last the rest of your life. It's right and natural for every child to be brought up in a *normal* home."

> —A "natural" mother's "unnatural" advice to unwed daughter Eleanor Parker, who doesn't want to give up her son for adoption, in *Three Secrets*

"Decent? Oh Mama . . . I surely am decent. Of course I'm a cheat and a liar and a thief . . . but I *am* decent."

> —Tippi Hedrin, bitterly, after living up to her mother's wishes for decency, in *Marnie*

"I don't ask much of *you* girl. Why can't you give me the respect I'm entitled to? Why can't you treat me like I would be treated by any stranger on the street!?"
"Because I am *not* one of your fans!"

> —A little mother/daughter chat between Faye Dunaway and Diana Scarwid in *Mommie Dearest*

"You were never a mother. You were a woman who had a daughter."

> —Susan Hayward making mama Bette Davis face the facts in *Where Love Has Gone*

"Working on the water heater again? I'm sorry to interrupt you, but it's been forty-eight hours since our last coition, my temperature's optimum, I'm ovulating, I have the pillows set up in the position Dr. Stenke wants us to try so that my cervix is placed better in the inter-vaginal seminal pool. You can watch TV if you get bored."

> —Practical Elizabeth McGovern eager for
> husband Kevin Bacon to reproduce in *She's
> Having a Baby*

"What's to know [about raising a child]? Whenever there's a problem I simply imagine how *you* would solve it. Then I do the opposite."

> —Harvey Fierstein to his mother Anne
> Bancroft on his abilities to raise a child in
> *Torch Song Trilogy*

"[Children] are impatient. I should know. I've had three chicks of my own. Only three, I grant you, Karen, but natural good manners told *me* when to put the plug in."

> —One-eyed monster Bette Davis who doesn't
> think much of her daughter-in-law or her six
> grandchildren in *The Anniversary*

"I'm an actor. I can do a father."

> —Ted Danson prepares for a real-life role in
> *Three Men and a Baby*

"What a pity my father didn't live to see me strong."

> —George Brent as a murderer who'd make
> any dad proud, in *The Spiral Staircase*

"When I was a little kid, maybe five years old . . . my mother used to say to me . . . she'd say, 'Don't get too close to people, you'll catch their dreams.' Years later, I realized I misunderstood her—*germs,* she said, not dreams. 'You'll catch their *germs.*'"

> —Martin Landau finally taking his mother's
> advice, in *Tucker: The Man and His
> Dreams*

"My husband and I have decided to give the advantage of our home to one of your foundlings. Of course, we wouldn't want one that cries."

> —Stipulating dowager Cecil Cunningham in
> *Blossoms in the Dust*

"Let me give you one word of fatherly advice—never give a sucker an even break."

> —Who's counting? W.C. Fields in *Poppy*

"One more piece of motherly advice—don't confide in your girlfriends."

> —Lucille Watson to Norma Shearer in *The Women*

"I think I know the best way to handle [Veda] . . . if you want her to do anything, hit her in the head first."

> —Jack Carson to mother Joan Crawford who fails to see her daughter's self-centered "weaknesses" in *Mildred Pierce*

"Girls like me weren't meant to be educated. We were made to have children. That's my ambition—to be a walking, talking baby factory."

> —Paula Prentiss, looking for a husband *Where the Boys Are*

"Now I can concentrate on my ambition in life: to get married and have babies. I'm selling myself as . . . a potential mother."

> —Connie Francis, *Looking for Love*

"There isn't any such thing in the world as a bad boy . . . but a boy left alone, frightened, bewildered . . . the wrong hand reaches for him."

> —Spencer Tracy in *Boys Town*

"Jennifer, be a bad girl."

> —Warlock Cecil Kellaway, to his daughter
> Veronica Lake, in *I Married a Witch*

"Once I had believed in my father, and the world seemed small and old. Now, he was gone, and I wasn't afraid to love him anymore, and the world seemed limitless."

> —River Phoenix remembering his father in
> *The Mosquito Coast*

"The stork that brought you must have been a vulture!"

> —Ann Sheridan to Pat O'Brien in *Torrid Zone*

"I didn't want to be born, and you didn't want me to be born."

> —The bitter truth from Bette Davis to mother
> Gladys Cooper in *Now, Voyager*

"Stretch marks are the badge of a real woman."

> —Kenneth Mars to daughter-in-law Molly
> Ringwald in *For Keeps*

"There was a dream I used to have about you and I. It was always the same. I'd be told that you were dead, and I would run crying into the street. Someone would stop and ask, 'Why are you crying?' And I would say, 'Because my father is dead and he never said he loved me.'"

> —Martin Sheen to his father Jack Albertson in
> *The Subject Was Roses*

"I love you both with all my heart. Do what you have to, to be happy in this life. There is so much beauty. Go well . . . my children."

> —Meryl Streep's dying wish to her son and
> daughter in *The Bridges of Madison
> County*

"Biology and the prejudices of others conspire to keep us childless."

> —And Nicolas Cage and Holly Hunter plan
> to do something about it, in *Raising
> Arizona*

"Even if the smallest part of you thinks you have to have a baby then you have to go ahead with it . . . it's easy, you'll have a baby and it'll be a boy with big blue eyes like yours and yellow hair and a little T-shirt and he'll be running out there—see him running? Jumping up and down? Mommy! Right? It's not hard."

—Elaine Kagan feeding childless Victoria
Foyt's fantasy of *Babyfever*

"Me? You don't care about me. All you care about is that bloody great army of children I'm supposed to work my guts out for . . . I can't even go to bed with you without one of them comes banging in the middle . . . I'm sick of living in a bloody nursery. Where the damn hell do I come in?"

—Daddy Peter Finch feeling a little left out of
his wife Anne Bancroft's baby-devotion in
The Pumpkin Eater

"My mother was going along the street when a procession of animals was passing by. There was a terrible crush of people to see them and unfortunately she was pushed under the elephant's feet, which frightened her very much. This occurring during a time of pregnancy . . ."

—A forgiving John Hurt explains his deformity
in *The Elephant Man*

"Why should I have to make some sad and decorous marriage just to have a child?"

> —Meryl Streep in *Plenty*

"Henry, I have a confession—I don't much like our children."

> —Katharine Hepburn, confessing, in *The Lion in Winter*

"If only Dad had the guts to knock Mom cold once."

> —James Dean in *Rebel without a Cause*

"Who taught you to be so cruel?"
"You did, Mama, you did. But you also taught me that if someone ruins your life, you can still feel love for them."

> —Kate Nelligan and Nick Nolte in *The Prince of Tides*

"She's like no other child . . . like no other child."

> —Beulah Bondi, anxious to give adoptive-parents-to-be Irene Dunne and Cary Grant the answer to their prayers in *Penny Serenade*

"When my little boy, Dimitri, died, everybody was crying. Me? I got up and danced. They said, 'Zorba is mad.' But it was the dancing—only the dancing—that stopped the pain. You see, he was my first. He was only three."

—Anthony Quinn in *Zorba the Greek*

"There isn't anything I wouldn't do to get you to free me of the curse of the Draculas—*I am Dracula's daughter!*"

—Gloria Holden growing weary of her father's legacy in *Dracula's Daughter*

"I've been spooked ever since I left my mother's tit."

—Harvey Keitel in *Eagle's Wing*

"Children shouldn't die before their parents. Parents should die first."

—Glenn Close in *The Stone Boy*

"Satan is his father, not Guy. He came up from hell and begat a son of mortal woman. And his name is Adrian."

—Sidney Blackmer sets Mia Farrow straight on her adorable, hoofed newborn in *Rosemary's Baby*

"I love her, but I wish she'd disappear."

> —Woody Allen's wish for his mother comes true, literally, in *New York Stories*

"What this family needs is discipline! I've been a pretty patient man—but when people start riding horses up the front steps and parking them in the library, that's going a bit too far."

> —A reasonable request by father Eugene Palette in *My Man Godfrey*

"She brought me up to be kind and thoughtful and ladylike, just like her, and I've been such a disappointment."

> —Vivien Leigh, thankful that her mother is dead, in *Gone with the Wind*

"You are my greatest disappointment. You lie, you shirk, you boast."

> —Shortsighted Robert Shaw to his "disappointing" son Winston Churchill in *Young Winston*

"I had a miscarriage . . . but I discovered macramé!"

> —Mary Garlington, easing her obvious emotional pain, in *Polyester*

"You're a disgrace to the name of Wagstaff, if such a thing is possible!"

> —Groucho Marx shows shame for his son in
> *Horse Feathers*

"I had a dream—*me.* My dream is like a nightmare, Mama. I dreamed I was a very old lady, but I was still doing the same old act. I was so ashamed of myself, I ran away, Mama—from the act, from your dreams because they only made *you* happy, and I want a dream of my own, my very own."

> —Ann Jillian's goodbye to Rosalind Russell's
> Mama Rose, in *Gypsy*

"It's such a relief not to have to worry about birth control."

> —Dinah Lenney on the joys of sex during
> pregnancy in *Babyfever*

"I look into your eyes and all I see are trashy dreams."

> —Concerned mother Mary Kay Place to
> daughter Laura Dern in *Smooth Talk*

"Either your education or your spanking has been neglected."

> —Barbara Stanwyck being scolded by Sam
> Levine in *The Mad Miss Manton*

"Dad makes fireworks because there's a sense of excitement about it—and my mother? Know why mother writes plays? Because eight years ago a typewriter was delivered to the house by mistake."

> —Jean Arthur explaining her parents' eccentricities to James Stewart in *You Can't Take It with You*

"Mom's got a good nose for people. You get one, standing year in, year out, behind a hamburger stand."

> —John Lund, sure his mother will like his new wife, Gene Tierney, in *The Mating Season*

"Have I been such a failure as a mother that I've raised a son with the morals of a snake?"

> —Disapproving Jacqueline Brooks to her son James Caan, *The Gambler*

"If I was bleeding out of my eyes, you'd make me go to school."

> —Jennifer Grey to her mother in *Ferris Bueller's Day Off*

"We McDonalds—we're high-tempered. We fight amongst ourselves, but let trouble come from outside and we stick together!"

> —Agnes Moorehead standing up for her brood in *Johnny Belinda*

"All right, tell me your worst paranoid fantasy. They drive off with the baby and the car and we never see them again? Maybe they hit a couple of convenience stores on the way and we end up on the *Geraldo Rivera Show* as the most gullible couple in America."

> —James Woods and Glenn Close sort out the possibilities after another couple agree to have a baby for them, in *Immediate Family*

"No one could ever love you like I love you."

> —Mother Anne Bancroft's dying words of warning to her son—never to marry—in *Honeymoon in Vegas*

"Unless I fulfill my destiny, my mother's labor pains were pointless."

> —Thoughtful Glenda Jackson in *Nasty Habits*

"Tell me the truth Mom, really, it's okay with me. Are you a serial killer?"

—Matthew Lillard, hopefully, to Kathleen
Turner, *Serial Mom*

"I'm very like father . . . Father is *my* job, not yours."

> —Katharine Hepburn, taking responsibility
> from her mother, in *A Bill of
> Divorcement*

"Dad loved Princeton. He was there nearly twenty years . . .
He certainly kept it looking beautiful. You've seen the grounds
of course . . ."

> —Irene Dunne, qualifying her father's
> "college days" in *The Awful Truth*

"Men like my father cannot die. They remain a living truth in
my mind. They are with me still . . . real in memory as they
were real in flesh."

> —Irving Pichel in *How Green Was My
> Valley*

"My old man . . . he was a corker!"

> —William Holden in *Picnic*

"Just because a woman meets a man in a barroom doesn't
mean he's your pa."

> —Ryan O'Neal, the last one to admit the truth
> to his daughter Tatum, in *Paper Moon*

"I have no time for this daddy stuff."

—Robert Loggia to son Richard Gere in *An Officer and a Gentleman*

"He's planning the rest of my life for me, and he's never asked me what I want. . . . I'm trapped."

—Robert Sean Leonard asking for help from teacher Robin Williams in *Dead Poet's Society*

"My father had become the whole world to me. When he died I had nothing. I was ten years old."

—Jodie Foster in *Silence of the Lambs*

"A few days ago, the whole family got together to discuss what to do for Mom . . . Taking into consideration her love, demeanor, the way she brought us up, the way she accepted our sweethearts, the fond memories, the happy hours . . . We decided to kill her!"

—The family's plans for Mama Bette Davis in *The Anniversary*

"A very common neurosis, particularly in this society, whereby the male child wishes to sleep with his mother . . . What puzzles me, Harold, is that you wish to sleep with your grandmother."

—Bud Cort, analyzed, in *Harold and Maude*

"The only good thing about divorce . . . you get to sleep with your mother."

—So gushes little Virginia Weidler to Norma Shearer in *The Women*

"I've forgotten how much that woman hates me, and how much I hate her."

—After Barbara Stanwyck's Christmas reunion with her mother fails in *Remember the Night*

"Mom died when I was three and I suppose Dad did the best he could. Instead of Mother Goose I was put to bed at night to stories of Babe Ruth, Lou Gehrig and the great Shoeless Joe Jackson . . ."

—Kevin Costner in *Field of Dreams*

"Veda, I think I'm really seeing you for the first time in my life and you're cheap and horrible."

—It's about time. Joan Crawford to her daughter Ann Blyth in *Mildred Pierce*

"I had a girl up here—a beautiful girl I'll probably never see again . . . and [Mama] fucked it up. She's ruining me, Sid, she takes up all my time. My practice is going to hell, my life is going to hell—I've had it, Sid. Something has got to be done! . . . I'm *not* putting her in a home. I'm going to kill her."

> —George Segal, at wit's end, wanting advice from his brother on deranged Ruth Gordon in *Where's Poppa?*

"Chip . . . Our mother is Charles Manson."

> —Ricki Lake finally catches on about *Serial Mom*, Kathleen Turner

"I don't like being an average girl from an average family."

> —Average Teresa Wright in *Shadow of a Doubt*

"My father was a . . . drunk, whore-fucker, bar-fighter, super masculine, and he was tough . . . My mother was . . . very po-etic, also drunk, and my memories about when I was a kid was of her being arrested nude."

> —Marlon Brando's cuddly memories of his parents in *Last Tango in Paris*

67

"I remember your hand as a boy. It was small and firm and dry."

> —Gunn Wallgren, upon holding the hand of his son's ghost, in *Fanny and Alexander*

"Dad, you're my father. I'm your son. I love you. I always have and I always will. But you think of yourself as a colored man. I think of myself as a man."

> —Sidney Poitier in *Guess Who's Coming to Dinner*

"A man who doesn't spend time with his family can never be a real man."

> —Marlon Brando in *The Godfather*

"Every fool with a dick can make a baby, but only a man can raise his children."

> —Larry Fishburne in *Boyz 'n the Hood*

"We taught you how to think, your mother and I, and if you make a mistake, it's our mistake too."

> —Lionel Barrymore sharing the guilt with son
> Mickey Rooney in *A Family Affair*

"Let me tell you, I am not a father figure . . . In fact, the only figure I intend being is a total stranger figure."

> —Cary Grant, upon inheriting Leslie Caron's
> brood in *Father Goose*

"Mommie said there are no monsters, no *real* monsters, but there are."

> —Carrie Henn, having nothing of her late
> mother's advice in *Aliens*

"And my own dear mama, wherever she is, God bless her and keep her safe from harm."

> —Buster Phelps praying for his mother in
> *Three on a Match*

"What do I need with a wife? I've got you, haven't I?"

> —Devoted James Cagney to his mother in *The
> Irish in Us*

"Where is my mother going away to, and why can't I go along? Please?"

> —Mickey Kuhn, at his mother Olivia de Havilland's deathbed in *Gone with the Wind*

"All I ever had is Ma."

> —James Cagney, who'd do anything for Ma, in *White Heat*

"You don't know what it means to be a mother! *I do!*"

> —Father Van Heflin to his wife in *Weekend with Father*

"My old lady's a dyke. Big deal."

> —Understanding daughter Jesse Solomon hears the truth in *Lianna*

"You're beginning to sound just like my mother!"

> —Lea Thompson, *Back to the Future,* and not understanding why her own son won't respond to her advances

"Finding new and preferably disgusting ways to describe a friend's mother was always held in high regard."

> —Richard Dreyfuss recalling his childhood in
> *Stand by Me*

"Dirk Bogarde never distempered *his* mother's bedspread."

> —Julie Walters to her gay son Gary Oldman
> in *Prick Up Your Ears*

"I see Molly every second weekend and during school vacations and we try to make the most of our time together. Sometimes I'm alright, but other times the pain of the loss is terrible. And then I think of something that Gram said to me . . . she said, 'Everybody knows you're a good mother.' "

> —Diane Keaton in *The Good Mother*

"As you grow older, my dear, you will learn that conventions are there because there is a need for them."

> —Lucille Watson to her daughter Barbara
> Stanwyck in *My Reputation*

"You noble . . . mothers bore the brains out of me."

> —Non-maternal Joan Crawford in *The
> Women*

"All I said was that our son—the apple of our three eyes, Martha being a cyclops—our son is a beanbag."

> —Richard Burton on his "blonde-eyed, blue-haired son" in *Who's Afraid of Virginia Woolf?*

"Mom is many things . . . normal isn't one of them."

> —Winona Ryder, speaking of Cher, in *Mermaids*

"Why don't you get some Chinese food for dinner? I've left your father. Love, Mom."

> —Veronica Cartwright's note to her son in *Valentino Returns*

"Ladies and gentlemen of the jury, look at that old woman there. How would you like to come home every night and find a potato sitting in your living room?"

> —George Segal, begging the courts for release from his horrid mother Ruth Gordon, in *Where's Poppa?*

"Your mother was a hamster and your father smelled of elder-berries."

> —Peculiarly rude insult to John Cleese in *Monty Python and the Holy Grail*

"Mother . . . is a bit of a problem."

> —Matricidal Tuesday Weld, enlisting the aid of sucker Anthony Perkins in *Pretty Poison*

"The first time you hear the word 'Daddy'—I don't care who you are—your heart just melts."

> —Cabbie Mario Joyner reassuring *Three Men and a Baby*

"Mom has been gone two years now. It's all right to have a little perfume in your life."

> —Robby Benson encourages his widowed father Paul Newman to date someone who smells nice in *Harry and Son*

"Mr. Rhodes, is there anything wrong with your wife? When she came to see me about Jimmy John I tried to discourage her. But when I told her that he was sullen, mean, and the worst student in summer school . . . a gleam came into her eye."

—Cary Grant, reminded of his wife's penchant for adopting troubled teens, in *Room for One More*

"My son does the cutest thing . . . My son has custody—my *father*—my *son* is four-and-a-half, my *husband* has custody, my *father* is dead . . . Tom Jr. is always firing everybody, you know? If he doesn't like what you're doing, he'll say to his babysitter, who's usually my friend Janette, who can't have kids of her own because of this thing . . . in her uterus. He'll say to Janette, 'You're fired, Janette,' just because she wants to put him to bed or something. And just today he fired me! 'On Christmas Eve,' I said, 'You're going to fire your own mother?' He said, 'You're fired' so . . . I'm fired."

—Deeply bothered mother Mia Farrow on the lam from her family in *Reckless*

"I don't have any privacy. It's like having children in the house."

—Jessica Tandy, equating servant trouble with motherhood, to her own son, in *Driving Miss Daisy*

"I opened my eyes and there I was in my mother's arms. She put me over her shoulder and burped me. Makes wonderful pies."

—John Wayne, remembering Mama in
Tycoon

"A man's best friend is his mother."

—Not a good thing to say—for Ralph Bellamy anyway—in *The Awful Truth*

"Mother? Mother? Where are you?"

—*Bambi* doesn't want to know the answer

"Him with those ears that only a mother could love."

—Hardly. After all, it's *Dumbo*

"Mom always had a way of explaining things so I could understand."

—Tom Hanks as *Forrest Gump*

"It's the next best thing to being a mother."

—Rebecca DeMornay, on "nannyhood" in
The Hand That Rocks the Cradle

"If we could bring the mothers of the various nations together, then there would be no more war."

>—Vanessa Redgrave in *Howards End*

"Miss Lora, I killed my mother."

>—Susan Kohner, a little too late for regrets, in *Imitation of Life*

"What do people have in common with mothers, anyway?"

>—Analyst Judd Hirsch trying to get through to mother-troubled Timothy Hutton in *Ordinary People*

"This is it, young Nathan, Jr.—you can just feast your eyes about, ol' boy . . . I'm gonna show you around. Looky here, young sportsman, that there's the kitchen area where Ma and Pa chow down. This here's the TV—two hours maximum, either educational or football . . . and this here's the dee-van, for socializing and relaxing with the family unit."

>—Nicolas Cage introduces his infant son to the niceties of white-trash living in *Raising Arizona*

"A mother—a *real* mother is the most wonderful person in the world."

—*Peter Pan*

"Poor father. How lonely and dark it must be for him at night, while we're at home by the fire."

—Freddie Bartholomew at his father's grave in *David Copperfield*

"I understand now! It's not *height* I'm afraid of—it's parents!"

—Mel Brooks in *High Anxiety*

"A man builds for his son. That's all he builds for."

—Broderick Crawford in *All the King's Men*

"And then one day when our first born son was put into my arms, he could see that the boy had inherited his own eyes, as they once were, large, brilliant and black."

—Joan Fontaine, finally happy, as *Jane Eyre*

"Babies? I can't even take care of a Chia Pet!"

—Winona Ryder, shuddering at the thought of motherhood, in *Reality Bites*

"How could something so small create so much of something so disgusting?"

> —Tom Selleck and his first diaper change, in *Three Men and a Baby*

"You try to live three miles from me and you won't live long, honey. You best keep running . . . and you know it. 'Bye baby."

> —Bonnie Parker's mother, who doesn't need intuition to tell her she'll never see her daughter alive again, in *Bonnie and Clyde*

"My mother—what you say about her—she was a woman, a servant woman who worked hard. She was a hard-working woman and it is not fair—not fair—what you say . . . I have her picture . . . I would like you to judge. I want you to tell me. Was she feebleminded? My mother? Was she feebleminded?"

> —Montgomery Clift, a witness at the *Judgment in Nuremberg*

"You've been alone so much, Belinda, but you're not going to be alone anymore. You're going to be a mother."

> —Music to Jane Wyman's ears, as *Johnny Belinda*

"I hate softness. My mother was soft. It killed her."

—Kirk Douglas in *Detective Story*

"May I have this dance . . . Mother?"

—John Lund acknowledging Olivia de Havilland as his mother in *To Each His Own*

"You don't know what it's like being a mother, Ida. Maybe [Veda] didn't turn out as well as I'd hoped she would when she was born, but she's still my daughter . . ."

—Joan Crawford as *Mildred Pierce,* bound and determined to stand up for her rotten daughter

"Mrs. Rhodes, I know you from way back. Every stray dog and cat finally makes its way to your home. You never ask them about *their* background."

—Laureen Tuttle trying to convince Betsy Drake to adopt a sullen teenager in *Room for One More*

"[You're not stupid], you're a man . . . you can learn to do the shopping for the family, maybe even do the dishes. But that doesn't make you a mother."

> —Lucille Ball to widowed father Henry Fonda in *Yours, Mine and Ours*

"I . . . put in a call to my mother. I said, 'I'd like to come home for the weekend and talk to you.' She said, 'What about . . . are you drunk?' I said, 'No, just lonely.' She said, 'Well, honey, I'm going to the Springs, but you can have the apartment. The cook will be there.' I said, 'Thank you, Mother' and hung up."

> —Lee Kinsolving's despair in *The Dark at the Top of the Stairs*

"He was never all Norman, but he was often only Mother."

> —Simon Oakland explains Mrs. Bates and son, in *Psycho*

"I wonder how a mother could call a boy Florenz."

> —Kay Medford to the one-and-only in *Funny Girl*

"He's a nice kid, really—in spite of his homelife. I mean, most kids would grow up neurotic, what with Martha here carrying on the way she does, sleeping till four in the P.M., climbing all over the poor bastard, trying to break down the bathroom door to wash him in the tub when he's 16 . . ."

> —Richard Burton, apologizing for less-than-motherly Elizabeth Taylor, in *Who's Afraid of Virginia Woolf?*

"If you lose a son, it's possible to get another. There's only *one* Maltese Falcon."

> —Sydney Greenstreet has his priorities, in *The Maltese Falcon*

"I thought I might get her once—just this once in the whole of her life—to publicly disagree with her mother. It'd save her soul if she did."

> —Burt Lancaster talking about gutless, ruined Deborah Kerr, in *Separate Tables*

" 'Mother. I am convicted. George.' "

> —Montgomery Clift wires his dear mother the bad news, in *A Place in the Sun*

"In all creation is there the female of the species who will not sacrifice her own life to protect the life she has conceived? Dark and terrible years between this woman and her son—but she protects him, even now, with her life. Her son will never know how deeply he is loved. She thinks he would be ashamed of her. I think he would kneel, and hold her to his heart."

> —Attorney Keir Dullea, not realizing he's defending his own mother, Lana Turner, for murder, in *Madame X*

"Your brother's children got no necks . . . Their fat little heads sit on their fat little bodies without a bit of connection."

> —And that's why Elizabeth Taylor thinks children are "no-neck monsters" in *Cat on a Hot Tin Roof*

"We had a son, 23 years old. I threw him out of the house last year. Pioutistic little humbug. He preached universal love, but he despised everyone. He detested my mother because she had a petty bourgeois pride in *her* son, the doctor . . . I grabbed him by the poncho, and I dragged him the length of our seven-room, despicably affluent, middle-class apartment and I flung him. Out. I haven't seen him since."

> —George C. Scott in *The Hospital*

"Mrs. King, throughout this grisly meal your son has been pelting me with cereal. I have taught him an object lesson, and, as you will observe, he doesn't like it. I guarantee that he will never throw cereal at me or anyone else again. Ever."

> —Impatient, baby-hating babysitter Clifton Webb, fighting cereal with cereal, in *Sitting Pretty*

"I had a lot of help—and I had a head-start over most of you fellas. I had a chance to pick my own parents."

> —Troubled adoptee Clifford Tatum Jr. getting his Cub Scout badge, and giving Betsy Drake and Cary Grant their due in *Room for One More*

"I should've given you to God the day you were born."

> —Hardly a blessing, coming from Piper Laurie to daughter *Carrie*

"You don't need a male. I mean, two mothers are absolutely fine."
"Really? Because I always feel very few people survive one mother."

> —Diane Keaton and Woody Allen in
> *Manhattan*

"I don't know how to feel about what you did. Maybe I never will. But I know you did it for me. I don't want to lose you again."

> —Jennifer Jason Leigh, on the secret that finally binds her to her mother, *Dolores Claiborne*

"My father grew up in the Great Depression—*his mother's.*"

> —Al Franken making sense of his rotting family tree in *Stuart Saves His Family*

"You smell like the toasted cheese sandwiches my mother used to bring me."

> —Anthony Perkins, who still hasn't come to terms with his mother—or her cooking—in *Psycho II*

"I won't insist he be tough . . . I won't insist he read the Marine Corps manual. Instead, I'll get him a set of Shakespeare. In short, I don't want him to be a sergeant . . . I want him to be intelligent, considerate, cultured and a gentleman."

> —Father-to-be John Agar lectures John Wayne on the qualities of a real man in *Sands of Iwo Jlma*

"For twelve years I've been forbidden to see my children, but I've seen the soul of D.H. Lawrence."

> —Janet Suzman on her sacrifice after eloping with the notorious author in *Priest of Love*

"Hey Dad? What happened in school today?"

> —Dudley Moore, to his son Kirk Cameron, after switching brains for a day, in *Like Father, Like Son*

"Strange to have a daughter who wouldn't go through with her wedding night. When I was her age, I'd go through with just about any old night."

> —Ellen Burstyn referring to her reticent daughter, Cybill Shepherd, in *The Last Picture Show*

"What a time we've had, Rosie. We'll never lack for stories to tell our grandchildren."

> —An understatement for Humphrey Bogart, to Katharine Hepburn, in *The African Queen*

"I saw her drink battery juice from your Honda."

> —It's going to take more than that for Alyson Hannigan to convince her father that *My Stepmother Is an Alien*

"I'm not talking mother to son. I'm talking shrink to shrink."

> —Psychiatrist Jessica Tandy to her analyst son Roy Scheider, and meaning business, in *Still of the Night*

"Really Papa, you'd think Mama had never seen a phone. She makes no allowance for science. She thinks she has to cover the distance by sheer lung power."

> —Little Edna Mae Wonacott exhibiting little patience for her loud-mouthed mother in *Shadow of a Doubt*

"He's awful damn good. I think I got the best one!"

—Happy father Nicolas Cage, after kidnapping his new son, in *Raising Arizona*

"What to you mean illiterate? My mother and father were married . . ."

—Joe Caits taking unnecessary offense, in
After the Thin Man

"I don't know when the war between my parents began, but the only prisoners they took were their children."

—It's how Nick Nolte begins the story of his life, in *Prince of Tides*

"I scared your daddy into getting rich, beautiful. You're not scary enough."

—Ellen Burstyn convincing her daughter Cybill Shepherd not to take any chances, and marry rich, in *The Last Picture Show*

"Adolescence is a time when people worry about things there's no need to worry about."

—Heinz Ruehmann comforts teen Gila Golan in *Ship of Fools*

"Everything is possible when seen through the eyes of youth."

> —Morton Selten revels in the wonders of youth in *The Thief of Bagdad*

"Say Dada—anybody can say Mama. Say Dada. Don't be a baby . . . say it!"

> —Robin Williams, eager to hear it from his infant son, in *The World According to Garp*

"I saw an old couple being visited by their children, and all their grandchildren, too. The old couple wasn't screwed up and neither were their kids or their grandkids . . . I don't know, you tell me, was this whole dream wishful thinkin'? Was I fleeing reality like I know I'm liable to do? . . . It seemed real. It seemed like us. And it seemed like our home. If not Arizona, then a land not too far away, where all parents are strong and wise and capable . . . and all children are happy and beloved . . ."

—Childless father Nicolas Cage dreams of a happy future for both him and his wife, in *Raising Arizona*

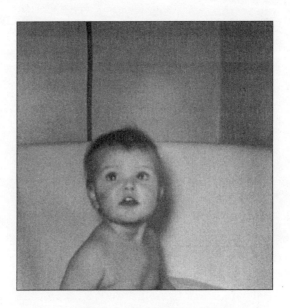

ABOUT THE AUTHOR

Jim Poling is a former film critic and film exhibitor. He lives in Brooklyn, New York with his son Jimmy.